Gotcha Goat

By Carolyn j Morris

Gotcha !
♡ Jcjmorris

Illustrated by Richard McNaughton

www.railfencebooks.com

Printed in Canada

ISBN 978-1-7753841-6-8

FIN 25 04 2023

Gotcha Goat

Gotcha Goat was an ordinary goat, curious and playful.
When Gotcha Goat was just a two month old kid,
she wriggled under the fence and frolicked in the grass.

Uh Oh!

When Gotcha Goat was a six month old doeling,
she squeezed between the gates and
ate the garden lettuce.

Uh Oh!

When Gotcha Goat was eight months old,
she jumped over the fence and wandered
into the sunflower field.

Uh Oh!

Every day after that, Devon and Taylor chased after her. And most days, Gotcha Goat stopped for the children to catch her. She liked when they hugged her around the neck and called her by name.

The longer they played Follow the Leader, the farther the trail led into the sunflower field. The sunflowers grew taller, almost reaching to the sky in the August heat and rain showers. Gotcha Goat was growing bigger and ran too fast for Devon and Taylor. That day, Gotcha Goat didn't stop for the children to catch up and hug her.

Uh Oh!

As the children followed their well-worn path back
through the rough, scratchy leaves and tall, strong
stem sunflowers, they made a plan.
Devon and Taylor set out to build a whatchamacallit
to help them keep up to Gotcha Goat's pace!

Ta-da!

Devon pulled the rope and Taylor pushed the cart. The wheels were a bit wobbly. Maybe that's why their mom had put the old stroller in the garbage!

The children attached the cart to Gotcha Goat
and she pulled Devon and Taylor, one by one,
through the sunflower field.

Soon word spread about Gotcha Goat and the
whatchamacallit. Friends visited to join the fun.

The other goats watched the excitement

from their pasture.

Summer was coming to an end and the children were starting school. It didn't stop them from wondering if Gotcha Goat could pull a toboggan in the winter.

Goat Definitions

Buck or Billy: adult male goat

Doe or Nanny: adult female goat

Herd or Trip: a group of goats

Kid: a young goat birth to six months

Buckling: a young male goat over six months

Doeling: a young female goat over six months and before motherhood

Kidding: the time when female goats give birth to their kids

Goat Milk: milk produced from a goat for human consumption

Goat Cheese: is made around the world and there are many different styles of cheese, from fresh and soft to aged and hard.

Goat Facts

⭐ Goats eat grass, hay, barley, peas, corn, oats, soybean, woody shrubs, and weeds.

⭐ Goats have no teeth in the front of the upper jaw.

⭐ Goats are raised for meat, milk and fibre.

⭐ Goats have rectangular pupils. They can see danger approaching from their peripheral vision. Their vision can be as much as 340 degrees.

⭐ Goats are intelligent, independent and curious.

⭐ Goats have a fur (hair) coat.

⭐ Goats usually live 12 - 16 years.

⭐ A goat is pregnant for 145 - 155 days (about 5 months).

⭐ There are about 300 distinct breeds.

⭐ Most goats don't require shearing.

⭐ Mohair, produced by Angora goats, is sheared twice a year.

⭐ Cashmere goats are raised especially for their undercoat of fine soft wool. It's sheared only once a year.

Sunflower Facts

⭐ A plant with a very tall stem and a single large, round, flat, yellow flower.

⭐ Each sunflower is actually thousands of teeny flowers.

⭐ The disk of a single sunflower contains up to 2,000 tiny flowers. All those tiny brown and yellow disks are tiny flowers, which can make thousands of seeds.

⭐ Sunflowers reproduce through pollination, with the support of pollinators, like bees.

⭐ Sunflower seeds are the fruit of a sunflower, which can be eaten or turned into an oil.

⭐ Sunflower oil is used as a cooking oil.

⭐ The flowers produce yellow dye.

⭐ The sunflower leaves are used as fodder.

⭐ Sunflowers are known for being happy flowers. They can make the perfect gift to bring joy to someone's day.

⭐ The sunflower is the national flower of Ukraine and is the state flower of Kansas.

⭐ During the day, the young sunflower follows the direction of the sun across the sky from east to west. This process is known as heliotropism.

⭐ Sunflowers are yellow. But they can also be red and purple!

⭐ Standard sunflowers usually grow 190 - 300 cm (6 - 10 feet) tall.

⭐ Giant sunflower varieties can grow 450 - 600 cm (15 to 20 feet) tall.

About the Author

Carolyn's country roots began on the family farm on the 10th Line of the old Nottawasaga Township. Carolyn j Morris has taught in both Toronto and rural communities for over 35 years. Now, along with author presentations throughout the year, she shares baby chicks and ducklings from March through June with the young and young at heart.

www.railfencebooks.com

About the Illustrator

Richard McNaughton is an award-winning artist whose works are hanging in private collections throughout North America and Europe. Working in both watercolour and acrylic, Richard's art reflects his love for the rural countryside, especially the Grey/Bruce area of Ontario. Richard and his wife, Nancy, live in the London area close to their grandchildren.

richardmcnaughton.wordpress.com